I0201492

Moon Over the Lost City

Poems of Nostromo

J Guenther

October 2018 edition

Wyzard Hill Press

MOON OVER THE LOST CITY

Copyright © 1999, 2018 J Guenther. All rights reserved.

Published by Wyzard Hill Press

Palos Verdes, California

No part of this publication may be reproduced, stored in a retrieval system, or transmitted in any form or by any means, electronic, mechanical, photocopying, recording, or otherwise, without the prior written permission of the copyright owner.

This book is sold subject to the condition that it shall not, by way of trade or otherwise, be lent, resold, hired out, or otherwise circulated without the publisher's prior consent in any form of binding or cover other than that in which it is published and without a similar condition including this condition being imposed on the subsequent purchaser. Under no circumstances may any part of this book be photocopied for resale.

This is a work of poetry. The characters, situations, and places are subjective images and do not necessarily represent reality.

For information leave comments at:

https://JGuentherAuthor.WordPress.com

Book and cover design by J Guenther. Typeset in:

CrimsonText-SemiBold.ttf: Copyright © 2010, Sebastian Kosch (sebastian@aldusleaf.org), with Reserved Font Name "Crimson".

IMFePIsc28P.ttf: © 2007 Igino Marini (www.iginomarini.com) with Reserved Font Name IM FELL DW Pica SC.

CinzelDecorative-Black.ttf: Copyright 2012 Natanael Gama (info@ndiscovered.com), with Reserved Font Name 'Cinzel'.

CC0 Cover images: "Blood Moon," ulrikebohr570. "Bangkok Skyline Silhouette," Thammarith Likittheerameth; modified

Printed in the United States of America

ISBN: 978-0-9974503-4-7

Sixth Edition: 2018

10 9 8 7 6

DEDICATIONS

To my teachers:

Gibson Reaves, Richard Condon, Dr. Julia McCorkle, Jeff Hoppenstand, Edith Battles, Anne Lowenkopf, Glad Esther Mitchell, Bill Barnett, Judy Sanger, Mrs. Keshishian, and all the others.

Special thanks to:

David Kenney, the entire South Bay Writers Workshop of bygone days, the Palos Verdes writing workshop, and Writers of Kern.

IN MEMORIAM
Peggy Connelly

Joe Tomasi

Vangie Maynard

FOREWORD

If you are that rare person who is curious about why or how poets write poetry, or if you just want to take advantage of every page you paid for, read on.

I wrote most of my poetry between 1989 and 1999 under the pen name "Nostromo," borrowed from the space freighter in the movie *Alien*, which took it from Conrad's novel of the same name. Some were written from inspiration; some were already in my mind upon waking. Others were written more deliberately, following a particular rhyme scheme. A few represent my own thoughts or feelings. Many were class exercises or sketches of imaginary people or situations. One or two are song lyrics, such as "Call of a Distant Song."

Some of these follow the older poetic forms. I now begin my poems as free verse. After looking the first draft over for potential meter or rhyme, I decide whether to finish it as a classical poem or not. Usually, I don't. Classical poems are in disfavor, now, in academia, most academics not having the patience to evaluate hundreds of badly written rhymed, metered poems each semester. They much prefer free verse, which has limits to its awfulness, at least in theory, as well as to its art.

I like *haiku*. It is possible to write a fairly decent *haiku* in English, although many artistic qualities of Japanese *haiku* are missing. The least important thing is the syllable count. For English *haiku*, I prefer a title and two rhyming lines of ten syllables each. I've posted a series of articles entitled "Why You (probably) Can't Write Haiku" on my blog:
https://JGuentherAuthor.wordpress.com

I hope you will enjoy these poems. If you do, please write a review and post it in a prominent place. I'll be very grateful.

J Guenther

Moon Over the Lost City

Silently, the fat moon rises from the forest
to gloat above the stones of Nydah-Venn.
Ghosts wander from pools of blackness
and slink along their customary ways,
murmuring their sins.

Hourly, 'til dawn glows on distant mountains,
a skeletal muezzin ascends the
last unfallen minaret
and croons his malison on those below:
"Too late! Too late!" the bony jaws intone.
Ten thousand voices cry out in return.
"Would have!" "Could have!" "Should have!"

No libertines haunt these granite avenues,
no fornicators and no thieves tread the
mossy stones of Nydah-Venn;
nor greed-bound merchants,
nor petty sinners.

This Gehenna of Regret is for those
who left something undone,
who let their joy escape,
devalued their heart's desire.

Those who lived their passion
have passed on,
never to haunt the paths and stony
pits of Nydah-Venn.

❦

The Pieces of the Puzzle of Her Life

Alice didn't seem to do much, her last five years. She made no friends, went nowhere, seldom had visitors or called anyone. At 97, she wondered why she still lived when the others were gone so long ago. When her youngest sister died, she said she was "Last of the Mohicans." She'd had twelve brothers. and sisters, all gone, now. She grew weaker. Dreams became reality, and reality, dreams. But I saw a change in her stories as she put together odd fragments of her life from years before. Some seen, some unseen. No new pieces, just working with the ones she had: At 95, she decided she'd been adopted. Could any parents treat their own child the way they'd treated her? She must have been adopted, she thought. But at 97, she decided they'd

The Pieces of the Puzzle of Her Life (cont'd.)

done about the best they could, with so many children, and said no more about being adopted. She asked me one day: "Have you heard from Cora (her mother) lately?" I

said, "No, not a word." "Do you suppose she's still in Cleveland?" "Well," I said,

"I don't think she's moved lately," "You're being rather vague,"

she noted. "Are you telling me she's gone?" "Well, as a matter of fact, she is," I said. She was silent for a moment, then said "You know, she must be gone. The last time

I was in Strongsville, Ward took me to see her grave, so she must be gone." She paused, then added: "I guess I never really took it in." She asked me again a few weeks

later if Cora were back on the farm. Cora had left Alice's father, Pat, and I guess she never "took that in," either. I replied that Cora was still in Cleveland. Later, she got a notion that I'd bought back the old farm at Hudson. She said that as soon as she was stronger, she was going back to the farm. She wanted to sleep in her old bedroom.

"How did you manage to buy it back? she asked, puzzled. "Oh, there was an

option in the deed," I said vaguely. "Please don't let them cut any more of

the woods," she said. When little, she'd played and dreamed there, in the

forest. After it was sold In the '40's, a lumber company had cut down those woods that had been her only refuge when she was a child. I assured her I wouldn't let

The Pieces of the Puzzle of Her Life (cont'd.)

them cut any more of the woods. She asked once more if Cora were back on the farm. This time I told her yes. She was delighted to hear that and said she was anxious to go home herself, after seventy years away. That was two weeks before she died, the day she put together the very last of the pieces of the puzzle of her life.

❧

Losing a Fur Friend

Anything short of forever
is never quite long enough.
So tough that one must leave,
the other stay and grieve.
Often it's ours to say goodbye,
and try to ease them on their way.
then stay and mourn the little pet
we will remember. We won't forget
we are the caretakers, given pets in trust,
better equipped to lose them
than they are to lose us.

❦

Red Balloon

A red balloon
breaking free
climbs the towering
clear blue sky
Where are you going,
so all alone?

❦

6

Be With Me

You're going to be with me now,
you're going to be my own.
So smile and be happy,
the sad days all have flown.
The bad dream now is over,
the night has come and gone.
Together you and I, love,
will see the silver dawn.
The darkness now has ended
as shadows flee the sun
of morning's new beginning,
for you and I are one.
You'll soon forget your sorrow
and learn to laugh again,
and put the past behind you
as though it's never been.
The school of love is out now,
the final lesson's done;
it's summertime forever
when you and I are one.

❦

Crestline

Snowflakes fall slowly
drifting among the pine trees
Silence holds me fast.

❦

Ninety Seven

She didn't die in the hospital,
She died a little here
and a little there, like most of us:

She died some when my father died;
And later when she stopped
going places and having friends over,
thought the house was too big.

She died in her daughter-in-law's
home when she stopped
going outside to walk.

She died in her apartment
when she stopped going
to the grocery herself, or
doing the crossword, or
fixing meals, vacuuming...

She threw her medicine away
once, by mistake;
Wouldn't go to the doctor
because she felt too weak.

She died in the retirement home
when she couldn't keep track of her pills,
stopped getting up for meals,
broke with a faithful friend.
She died in the board and care home
when she wanted to stay in bed all day,
stopped reading and watching TV. ➽

Ninety Seven (cont'd.)

She died in the nursing home
when she could barely sign her name.
She died in the last board and care,
when she no longer always knew
who she was talking to...
Her dreams became real
and her reality, a dream.
"We went to Czechoslovakia last
week. The food? Oh, it was fine,
but the beer wasn't so good.
No, we didn't need passports,
we just got on the plane."
I treasured what ability remained:
to raise a glass of milk and drink it,
to say "Thank you for coming
to see me," and "How are the boys?"
to say goodbye, or finally just to nod
her head silently on the pillow.
And when the last bit died in the
hospital, there was just enough left
to cry over, but not enough to want
to hold back the darkness.

❦

Heart's Desire

Here there be dragons
here be forces dire,
here in the Land
of Heart's Desire.
We hold no shield,
a short, rusty sword,
only, in our hand
to pierce the darkness.

We fight more fear than foe.
Victory will be fleeting,
yes, and well we know
that laurels soon wither,
here in the Land
of Heart's Desire.

But each new day
our diadem shall be,
and though our bodies
must tire in the end
and turn to sand,
even so, remember
that bravery is love,
here in the Land
of Heart's Desire.

❧

The Cactus of Love

Oh, I climbed up the Cactus of Love jest fer yew..
Oh, that thorny ol' Cactus of Love jest fer yew.
When I got to the top, 'twas a heck of a view,
But I suddenly knew, gal, that yew were untrue.
Oh, I should'a known better, but hadn't a clue.
Now I'm biddin' yew goodbye, adios and adieu,
Fer it's time I was gone, gal, I'm long overdue,
Now I'm cryin' an' moanin' an' feelin' so blue,
'Cause I'm dreadin' the slidin' that I gotta do
Goin' back down that cactus, A-Ooh! A-A-Ooh!
I ain't never ever gonna climb it anew...
Unless I meet someone who reminds me of you...
So now, fellers, be wary, whatever you do,
Or that Cactus of Love, it'll puncture you too.
An' the day that you climb it's a day you will rue.
Don't go climbin' that cactus, no matter for who!

꙰

Elfin Evocation

After midnight,
elves beckon
from between
moon-shadowed
ferns, to dance me
clad in moonbeams
on dew-spangled grass
until the dawn.

꙰

Coronets and Croquet Sets *

Divoted doll, dancing down
the nine times running Meuse,
Palliasse grandly
mansions set before the Stroker.
What does it mean, Oleander Skate?
Calliope Strain, what gave
our hearts some rest?
Commerce gladly with
wintered silks and bowls,
(If Leviathan had conquered
one more summer pearl...)
Hoops and drains, hoops and drains!
Liquidated in myrrh,
that beside my one-time River Run,
There might come again another Sun.

* A denizen of Cafe Voltaire once
suggested certain letters here, mostly
vowels, have been suppressed:
Oleander Skate = Alexander the Great?
Palliasse ~ Pagliacci.
Hoops & drains = hopes & dreams.
Otherwise, River Run = life?
Stroker = an oversize auto engine.

❦

Platonic

She asked me
for a platonic hug,
And I complied.
It was several
hours before I could feel
anything again.
I wonder if I should have
offered her, instead, a
pile of ashes, grey
powdery fluff? Or a stack of
brown-edged hardware receipts
from 1968? Or some dry,
yellow leaves,
blowing in a November wind?

❦

Halloween Artist

She sat, poised, pen in one
hand, paring knife in the
other, stretched long
legs and smiled at the pumpkins
coaxing jack o' lantern faces
to appear, not so much carved, as just
eager to meet her.
That night, a small, wicked spheroid
grinned at me from the top of the
stairs, fangs from ear to ear, eyes glowing.
Beside it, a larger Jack cowered and rolled
his flickering eyes in terror.

❦

Arms Closing

I shut my eyes as my arms closed
and closed
and closed
around her.
Just as I'd begun to think they were empty,
my arms pressed within them
her small, lithe shape,
more precious for having briefly seemed
to have flown away,
for the long delay
before being found.
Two arms never seem enough
to hold her.
My heart knows it can't contain her,
but still it opens
and opens
and opens
to embrace her,
always wondering
until the last second
if she's really there.

❧

The Runner

Beat on, foolish heart,
take me far away from here—
the wind dries my tears.

❧

The Gravity of the Situation

Mercury dashed around the Sun, and the Sun, seeing that he drew no nearer, wondered why. "Mercury, I can see that you are drawn to me. You've been dancing around me for billions of years. Why do you stay 'way out there? Don't you find me attractive?

Mercury smiled, but continued to revolve around her. "Oh, yes," he said, "very attractive. So much so, that I have to keep running at 300 megafurlongs per fortnight just to keep my distance."

The Sun pouted and said "But why don't you come a little closer?"

And Mercury replied: "You've given me quite a fever even at this distance. If I came any closer, I'd find myself burning up, And I'd have to run even faster to keep from falling."

"What would be so bad about that?" the Sun asked. "Don't you think I am bright and beautiful?" Her voice quavered a tiny bit.

Mercury kept jogging by...and by...and by, in his unending orbit. "Yes," he said, "You are beautiful, and it's not a lack of brightness that makes me try not to fall. If I joined you down there, I would be totally lost in you. There would soon be no more Mercury, and where would that leave both of us?"

The Sun smiled and said, "Well, I suppose you're right. But perhaps you'll change your mind, someday."

❧

Distances

Grey clouds over an olive sea
flecked and rimmed with foam
like icing from a cake
that will never be.
Intermittent winter rain
spatters the windshield
before rubber-edged
metronomes wipe it away.
Click, click.
Tick, tick.
Tick, tock.
Click, clock.
Less than five score miles between us,
but the mirror and the radio remind me
that distances are measured
in more than miles.

The Pain Train

I dreamt I trudged in the sun along a railroad track, my old boots scrunching in the gravel beside knee-high weeds, straps on my pack pressing deep, sweat running down my back. I wished I could put my burden down or trade it for someone else's.

A lark sang sweetly all this time. "Easy for you to sing, bird, you aren't carrying my heavy pack of troubles and fears," I told him.

I felt a throbbing in the earth. I dropped my pack and put my ear to the cold steel rail. I heard the far away scream of metal wheels, engines groaning down the line. This was one big train coming.

Soon four locomotives snaked 'round the bend, huffing, chugging and pulsing. On and on they came, pulling a longer and longer string of cars. The sound was in the air, in the ground, and in the weeds behind me. The lark was silent now.

The first engine roared past. I covered my ears. The engineer took off her cap and waved it. She had no hair at all. I waved back, and she smiled, then put her cap back on and looked straight ahead.

The next engine came, and the next. Then the first boxcar, one of many, all alike. One...two...three...four...five... I was up into the hundred-and-somethings when I realized these cars were filled with pain, pain in crates and boxes, bales and bins. I sat among the weeds and tried to count but finally just closed my eyes and felt the throbbing as the train load of pain went by.

When the air grew still, I opened my eyes. The lark was back in business. I looked around for my pack, but couldn't find it. I found one an awful lot like it, but it was too small and light to be mine.

❦

THE BOTTOM LINE

Under the fluorescent company sky,
his feet trod the corporate grass so grey:
Left right
left right
left right.
Suited, tied, and leather shod,
he marched expressionless down
the corporate corridors,
undancing,
smiling only when some column
of numbers summed
to more than
or less than
or the same as
another. He worshiped the corporate gods,
heart
and mind
and soul.
The bottom line became more
important than life.
Man-made materials plastic'd away his
sense of sin. Competitors, committees
spread the blame;
options and profit sharing
anesthetized his heart...
Until one day, the company downsized
his job and upsized its profit, just one
of several important
bottom lines
he'd never
considered.

❦

"Twue Wub"

Love is not
a feeling, he says.
Yeah, right.
We all know how
unimportant feelings are.
Heck, I don't want
to feel them anyway.
What a relief:
Love is
just a head trip away,
in either direction.
[Someday
I'm going to
write a book called
"How to Recognize
Bullshit
When You Hear It."
I plan to have
a whole chapter titled
"Love is Not a Feeling."]

❦

A Tear for Olaf

"I'm fine," he said, looking at my eyes.
"We had good times, but now she doesn't
want to see me anymore.
I suppose I'll miss her.
I don't feel bad, though. I've got no
resentments, no regrets, no tears. It's
over, that's all.
She got her stuff; I got mine.
The only thing we couldn't find was
Olaf, the teddy bear I bought her
on our second date.
You know what's funny?
I think about that little bear,
lost in a small,
dark box somewhere, and
I think about how lonely
he must be...
But I'm fine," he said
and suddenly turned away.

❦

Hindoo Rope Trick*

Did I tell you about Mr. Gupta?
He is from India.
I hanged him over a year ago,
you know, hanged him in my
window with a rope.
You could see him if
you walked by and looked up.
But nobody ever does.

Yes, my room does smell strange.
It is very-very warm there,
and his leaves get plenty of sun,
so sometimes he is blooming
in ten or twelve
places at once,
pretty pink flowers,
with a scent like incense
and chocolate.

❦

* "Mr. Gupta" is a Hindoo rope plant (Hoya carnosa)

trust

i must tell you,
tell you i
can shoot an
apple off
your head.
i, will tell,
tell you not
to worry about
being pierced
by an arrow, here..
or here...or
even
down here.
where are you
going? i must
tell you...

❦

The Goblin On The Stairs

I'd been sick, the night
my father tap-danced up the stairs
I decided whatever was coming
had more feet and legs
than any human,
and I began to cry,
thinking a monster was
coming to get me.

❦

Sail Away on My Silver Dream

Come, sail away on my silver dream,
cast off the hawsers of Care,
leave all your troubles and sail away
over the ocean with me.

Come, sail away on my silver dream,
let the wind blow through your hair.
Feel the sun and the salt water spray;
know what it's like to be free.

Come, sail away on my silver dream,
breathe in the fresh briny air.
Let your heart soar on the wind today,
over the sapphire sea.

❦

Invisibility

In first grade, I learned that school
was a place where bigger kids
could do anything they wanted to you,
and who knew lots of ways to cause pain,
and didn't care if you cried.

In second grade I learned that if I could make
the bigger ones laugh, they might not punch me,
or if they did, couldn't do it quite as hard.

In third grade I learned that some of the nuns
were the meanest kids of all.

In fourth grade I learned to make myself
invisible, became a dodge-ball expert:
I'd never scream and run away from the ball.
I'd stand just inside the circle, fold my arms,
and look uninvolved.
Often, by the time they noticed me,
it was too late. Eventually,
I became permanently
invisible.

❦

Imprisoned Love

The tighter your grasp,
the less bird you'll discover
when your hand opens.

❦

Blue Fuzzy Blues

I got the blue, fuzzy blues, since you left me all alone.
I got the blue, fuzzy blues, since you left me on my own.

Oh, since you left me, Honey, I've lost a lot of weight.
There's tears upon my pillow an' tears upon my plate.
'Cause I can put the trash out, an' I can pay the rent;
An' I can fix the Chevy, but can't cook worth a cent.

A good thing I'm not hungry: I'm almost out of food.
I really should go shoppin', but jest ain't in the mood.
Open the refrigerator, here is what I see:
Blue and fuzzy groceries, a-lookin' back at me.

There's a blue fuzzy turnip, an' some blue, fuzzy cheese.
There's some blue fuzzy carrots with hominy an' peas,
I got blue, fuzzy onions, I got blue, fuzzy rice.
I got blue mashed potatoes an' a fuzzy pizza slice.

Got blue and fuzzy peaches, got blue and fuzzy bread.
I don't fix nothin' fancy, eat junk food stuff instead.
Oh, breakfast is a Twinkie™, an' lunch an Eskimo Pie™;
For dinner there's a DingDong™, an' then I sit an' cry:

Got oodles o' fuzzy noodles, an' a blue apple core;
Got a blue and fuzzy melon, an' pickles by the score.
I miss your cookin, honey, miss your lovin', yes I do.
Oh, I'm afraid my DingDong's™ gettin' blue and fuzzy,
too!

❦

All About Leather

It's not the destination that's important; it's
the road. Figure out the road, and eventually
you'll understand the journey.
And to know the road, you must walk it without
leather, for the road has texture, and
the texture is the road. You'll never feel
the road through leather.
To learn smooth, first learn rough;
to know about soft, try hard; before
cool, hot; before moist, dry.

Byron Woolsey always had leather, top grain
material. He was proud of his leather, and
his friends were of the same sort,
who never had to feel the road beneath them.
Instead of road, he learned leather.

And when the leather went away, when his feet
hit rough for the first time, his bloody footprints
led straight to the ditch, where there is no texture,
and no road, and no destination.

❦

Clouds

Vapor galleons
slowly sail the Sea of Air—
majestic shadows.

❦

Two Brown Eyes & a Smile

When you looked at me and smiled,
it was like being curled up
in front of a fireplace after an hour in a blizzard.
It was like the sun rising after the longest night,
like a hundred warm arms encircling me,
like someone had lit my lamp again,
after it had blown out on a long, dark road.

❧

Her Journal

Somewhere in a sunless heart,
a graphite torch lights the way,
shining on a bone-white page.
The black point leaves behind
Illumination
where it touches the paper,
letting in the moonlight,
to brighten shadowed,
shadowed corners of her mind
with hope of dawn.

❧

Relativity

After she smiled,
truth was only "I love you."
All else became lies.

❧

Ignition

In the cold, still hours before dawn,
Vapors vent from tanks of liquid sun,
as I stand waiting on the pad,
Gantry-tethered and solitary.
She comes alone from far across the tarmac,
White-suited, helmet gleaming under one arm,
Watching me with star traveler eyes.
The countdown has begun.
My turbines scream silently as she approaches.
White ice crystals flake and whirl down my sides.
Soon ice will turn to fire:
Cryogenic hydrogen and oxygen
will mix and burn,
Releasing power beyond her dreams.
Just at the sun's first light, she smiles at me.
Thunder takes the morning,
and I am torn away from the earth.
The world around me shakes.
I soar Everest-high in the blink of an angel's eyes,
ascendant in the bright dawn of the heart.
Burning like a star myself,
I rise to greet my brother Sun
and roar beyond the stratosphere,
past the point of no return.
Not too late to climb the gantry,
not too late to come aboard,
courageous rocket-rider.
Come aboard! Come along!
Fly with me forever,
Join me on a journey to the stars.

❦

Piano Strings

There's no escaping
the sound of the piano:
Clear and stark,
its notes ring truth into your soul.
Sadness, joy, and rain,
or sunny days of summer,
sounded out
in tones that tear your heart.
Simple as a tear on a cheek,
pure as the face of a sleeping child,
lonely as the whistle of a distant train,
deep as a dark blue mountain lake.
Tonight, my piano plays for you;
the melody's about a wish I made,
the lyric from the longing of my heart,
a song of faint hopes concerning you.

❦

Autumn Night

Moon takes center stage,
her silver voice rising clear—
Night's prima donna.

❦

Rhoum-Ga-Boom

Wind on the water, sighing in the reeds;
Southward a-winging the wild bird speeds;
Honk of the gander and cry of the loon:
Soon will come the evening of Rhoum-ga-boom.

Shaman in the village reads all the signs:
Falling stars at night and frost in the pines,
Settles on the night of the next full moon
for the annual festival, Rhoum-ga-boom,
Rhoum-ga-boom.

As stars pierce the dusk on the fated day,
Shaman chants softly and begins to sway.
People gather 'round in the growing gloom,
Waiting for the opening of Rhoum-ga-boom,
Rhoum-ga-boom, Rhoum-ga-boom.

The pale moon arising lights up the sky
As people join in in the shaman's cry.
Slowly, softly, they begin to croon
Traditional music of Rhoum-ga-boom,
Rhoum-ga-boom, Rhoum-ga-boom,
Rhoum-ga-boom.

Primitive liquor in pottery bowls
Stirs up a fire in primitive souls.
Build a great fire, light it, and soon
Drums mark the opening of Rhoum-ga-boom,
Rhoum-ga-boom, Rhoum-ga-boom,
Rhoum-ga-boom, Rhoum-ga-boom.   ➠

Rhoum-Ga-Boom (cont'd.)

Naked flesh gleams by the light of the fire.
Dancing, leaping, higher and higher,
Faster and faster they dance to the tune
Of the ritual music of Rhoum-ga-boom,
Rhoum-ga-boom, Rhoum-ga-boom,
Rhoum-ga-boom, Rhoum-ga-boom,
Rhoum-ga-boom.

Shaman holds aloft a mottled blue sphere,
Throws it in the flames as the people all cheer.
Thund'rous explosion and pyrotechnic plume
Start the final chorus "Mushroom go boom!
Mushroom go boom! Mushroom go boom!
Mushroom go boom! Mushroom go boom!
Mushroom go boom!

All around the embers the people find room
To dance horizontally beneath the moon,
Celebrating ancient planetary doom,
At post-Apocalyptical Rhoum-ga-boom,
Rhoum-ga-boom, Rhoum-ga-boom,
Rhoum-ga-boom...

❦

Spring Steel

"What's the matter?" she asked.

A vague discontent had grown
from nothing in particular,
formed a ball
that rolled around my mind,
then trundled down
the brain's steel chutes and ramps,
until it found a conduit to my heart.
BOOM!!
There, the discontent became
a restlessness,
a nameless, formless longing.

She sneezed and sniffed and said,
"It's Spring!"

"It's Spring. That's what's the matter."
April caught me unaware.

❦

The Blind Man Remembers Stars

The Blind Man turned his ancient head
and spoke toward where I'd been
a moment before.
"I almost remember stars," he told me.
"I think I remember seeing them
on a cold winter night...
Cold...so cold...
and they sparkled, shining high, high up,
like silver nails driven into a velvet ceiling...
Far away...so far away...
At least, I think I remember..."
he said, his voice fading, then added,
"I remember love like I remember stars."

❦

Courtyard

Beside the fountain's
splashing water,
the bright pink azalea watches.

❦

Reflection

Sky and pines ripple
on silent, spreading circles:
Cool pond in shadow.

❦

Argent Dragon

I rose mid-summer's day as royal morning slowly dawned, and barefoot ran where incense brook flows into silver pond. Fresh morning air slipped sweetly, coolly soft across my skin. Arriving at the pond, I stripped and swiftly dove therein.

I vaguely could remember that I'd dreamt the night before, a dream of something wicked—I remembered nothing more. "A dream is just a dream," I said, "'Twill vanish with the day." I swam until the water washed the memory away.

I later sat and let the wind and sunlight dry my hair, and tossed a pair of pebbles in the quiet water there. I stood and watched the sparkling, perfect circles start to grow, reflecting like my life across the water, to and fro.

But then I looked straight down into the waters of the pool, and saw beneath the surface an enormous scarlet jewel: the red eye of a dragon watching me from down below. I shuddered as my hairs stood up on head and hand and toe.

Too petrified to run, I knelt and saw his mighty jaws, enclosing teeth like swords, his unearthly limbs and claws: a dragon all of silver slowly swimming towards the sky, arising up to meet me as he winked one crimson eye.

He stopped there as he surfaced and he stared at me again. I shivered still in terror, knowing how close I had been to this enormous creature as I took my morning swim, and wondered why he'd let me go—a dragon's playful whim?

⇨

Argent Dragon (cont'd.)

Before my eyes I saw the dragon form begin to fade, to vanish from the crystal pool within the mossy glade. and as his image faded, then, I asked him for his name. but if he had an answer true, the answer never came.

"Whence came you, evil dragon? From some cavern 'neath the stream?"

"Not I," the dragon whispered, "I have come from in your dream."

I reflected for a moment, then again my clothing donned, and from that morning forward, swam no more in Silver Pond.

❦

First Time

She hid behind the lectern,
clutching her poem tightly,
as if it were a figleaf,
and she, Eve.
It was her first time reading,
and she sped through her poem,
streaking from stanza to stanza,
stopping only to breathe and blush.
She may have had clothes on,
but she knew
that her heart and soul
were truly naked.

❦

Erosion

A tear crossed your cheek,
Cut a canyon in my heart,
When I saw you cry.

❦

Barefoot

Summertime lover:
hand to hand
and cheek to cheek,
grass beneath our feet.

❦

Heffalumps

The great, thundering, two-ton beasts
crested the hill beside where we played.
They trumpeted, roared, and hissed,
passing noxious gases as they ran,
by ones or twos, in packs,
some grey, some white, some brown.
"Heffalump! Heffalump!" we cried
in mock terror, and ran barefoot
in search of a place to hide
till the hideous creatures
had trundled over the next hill,
their metal hearts beating,
tires whining, exhaust pipes farting.
Today, we ride over hill and plain,
surrounded by such creatures,
looking out at the road ahead
from inside, through the eyes
of one of these fearsome beasts.
Hands gripping the wheel tightly,
feet pumping the pedals,
imagining that we are in control,
when actually
we have been eaten by heffalumps.

❦

Loss

An empty place, where only grasses wave
No stone, no name, upon my father's grave.

❦

A Student's Death (J.M.)

Goodbye, beloved of our hearts;
your story ended all too soon.
The last chapter, penned far away from us,
ended at a comma,
forever now unfinished in our hearts.
Should we turn the empty pages,
and pencil in what might have been,
all our hopes and dreams for you?
Instead, we search for shreds of consolation
in earlier chapters, those few completed pages
accepted by the Editor as enough...

The ink now runs and blurs
as I write on tear-spattered paper...
I long to put away my pen
and write no more.
Could we hold dear
your lost, unwritten chapters,
and give no value to our own,
as precious to you, perhaps,
as yours to us?

And so we go on,
until the Editor chooses
to accept our manuscripts as done.
Our remaining chapters,
lived and written well,
shall be our last gift to you.
Each of them shall start and end
with mention of your name,
forgotten never, loved forever.

❦

Lies For Sale

Lies for sale! Lies for sale!
Get your lies here, fresh lies!
All shapes, all sizes, all colors of lieses.
There's nothing can make you feel better,
quicker than nice, fresh lies!
Try these on for size:
The US government doesn't have enough
power to deal effectively with drugs/
pornography/ pollution/ firearms/
illegal immigration/religious fanatics,

And so you must give up just
a teeny bit of your rights
(and a bunch of your cash)
so the poor, weak, benign government
can deal with these awful problems.
And we've got the tapes to prove it—
just give us a couple of weeks to make copies.

Lies—fresh lies! Get your nice fresh lies!
(Studies have shown that the words
"studies have shown"
are followed by a lie 93.7% of the time.)

Oh, yes, and sanitize, colorize, deodorize
with some nice word-lies! Get your new alibis!
Trivializing, saccharizing, neutralizing word-a-lizer:
If we call it shrdlu, shrdlu still happens,
but it won't stink. No shrdlu! I shrdlu you not!
I was born under the Sign of the Etaoin, myself.)
Oh, get your lies before the supplies dries!

❧

Medicine Woman

Someone stole my heart.
She took it away while I was dreaming,
and carried it back in a deerskin bag
to the distant valleys of her own country,
a warm, green land of flowers and honey,
where Feelings rule over Intellect,
far from my home
in the cold, windy mountains of Logic.

What she did to my heart there, I do not know;
some strange process, some sweet magic
of drums and fire and incense made
from purple flowers,
that changed my heart
and made it ache to take up the beat
of hers, pressed close, and echo the drums
of that land far away,
where someone took my heart.

❦

Summer

Sun and butterflies
dance 'round
the yellow roses—
summer in my heart.

❦

The Pool Player

Who was it said: "God doesn't play dice with the universe?" Maybe it was Einstein. Actually, I think the reason God doesn't play dice with the universe is that He much prefers pool.

Only, in God's case, 15 balls aren't enough to make it interesting, so at the time of the Big Bang, God's one and only cue ball struck a polydimensional triangle of 680 times 2 to the 256th numbered balls, and set the whole thing in motion.

Some of the solid atomic balls turn into stripes when they bounce off a cushion and become energy. After a few more bounces, some of the balls sink in the side pockets called "entropy."

This game has been going on for several billion years, and I don't think anybody else is going to get a turn. God called all His shots while He was chalking up, and He's going to clear the table on the break.

You and I are just billiard balls on God's green felt table, and maybe what seems like free will to us is like the nap on the felt to God—nothing that a little chalk can't handle...And just because you get sunk doesn't mean the game is over: Some say God once disguised himself as a One Ball, crossed the table, and let Himself be caromed into a pocket with everybody watching. Imagine their surprise when He popped out again two days later...

But I didn't see it, myself. If He's come back to the table since, He evidently doesn't wear the same number or do the same trick more than once.   ⇒

41

The Pool Player (cont'd.)

Right now, I've just been part of a 1,376,024 ball combination shot off 3,879 cushions, maybe more, And I'm feeling chipped and surprised I can still roll. I've seen myself heading for a pocket more than once, only to be hit by another ball and bounced out to the middle of the table at the last second. Ouch, is all I can say. From the point of view of the balls, pool is a painful game.

❦

Night Into Day

Faint mention of your name was magic,
once, that brought me sleep and dreams
beneath the stars.
Your distant heartbeat whispered "Peace;"
a memory of your touch caressed my soul.

Time to sleep, now, time to dream,
but there is no night—
a new sun has risen in the midnight sky:
Desire, shrieking with the power of a star,
humming, throbbing, pulsing, shattering
the night.

Near dawn, I find the faint moon
of Hope has set, never to rise again.
I sleep, certain, somehow, that another
has already claimed you.

❦

The Room Nearest the Door

In the nursing home,
the room nearest the door
is for those who will die the soonest—
so the gurney can squeak
the shortest path to the door,
disturbing as few as possible of those
who will pass on not quite so soon.
One day, I visited a friend
in that fortunate room
farthest from the door.
I had steeled myself for the sound
and smell of those whose minds
had gone on ahead of their bodies
that clutched at me from wheelchairs,
as I walked the endlessly ending corridors
past the room nearest the door.

As I passed the room that day,
I looked in, whether I wanted to or not.
There was a woman of many summers
lying there, motionless.
Beside her bed, an equally aged man
sat quietly, bent forward,
his head gently near her arm,
as if listening for some word
she'd never say again, now.
No sound came from her
as she slept away the last hours
of her last winter.
Nor any sound from him
as he spent the final hours with
one he'd known when she was young,   ⇨

44

The Room Nearest the Door (cont'd.)

perhaps the only person who
remembered him as youthful.

Soon, he'd put his arm out in the night
and feel it fall
on an empty place beside him.
Soon, he'd know that vague feeling
that she was still
somewhere,
because every other time she wasn't there,
she'd gone
somewhere.

I wished I had a camera,
to capture and keep forever
the beauty and sadness
in the room nearest the door.

❧

Sandalwood

She sits naked on the floor,
caress-sized breasts hidden
behind the guitar she plays.
Her hair, soft and dark,
falls to her pale, bare shoulders.
Her legs are crossed beneath her;
small bare feet project to either side
of the perfect roundness of her bottom,
displaying the neat progression of her toes.
She smiles at me more with her eyes
Than with her teeth.
My heart reaches toward her.
It's ten o'clock on a summer evening,
and I have lit some Indian incense.
The fragrant smoke rises, swirling,
dancing sweet arabesques to the ceiling,
sometimes curling in my direction,
beckoning, calling me from my page,
inviting me to join the wild dance
of Beauty's celebration.

❧

Stiki-Wik

My friends, I'm gonna talk to you about glue. Not just any ol' glue, but the 8th wonder of the modern world, the all-time glue, the glue of glues, the glue than which there is no whicher.

Friends, you can mend pottery, you can mend glass, you can mend leather, you can mend wood. You can mend anything from a broken pot to a broken pitcher.

You can even mend that plastic that's smoother and slipp'rier than a politician. And the name of this marvelous stuff is Stiki-Wik.

You can fix 'most anything with Stiki-Wik: It bonds, seals, glues, sticks, fixes, mends, caulks, and adheres real quick!

An' metal, let me tell ya 'bout mending metal with Stiki-Wik. You got a broken hinge? Stiki-Wik it cousin! You got a broken manifold? Stiki-Wik it, Sister! You got a broken con rod? Stiki-Wik it, Brother!

Stiki-Wik can mend anything, my friends. Stiki-Wik it and it'll stick together like Damon & Pythias, or Currier & Ives, or Laurel & Hardy. (Not like Gilbert & Sullivan; they hated each other.)

If the ancients had had Stiki-Wik, then the Sphinx would still have a nose, the Venus de Milo would be able to hug, the Winged Victory of Someplace would have a head on her shoulders, the Acropolis and the Parthenon would be together instead of apart.

Yes, Stiki-Wik can fix anything whatsome-who-so. Almost. Pretty near. Just about. Well, for the sake of accuracy in prevarication, I must admit there is one thing that Stiki-Wik can't fix, and that is a broken heart.

If Stiki-Wik could mend broken hearts, you can bet your bum I'd be home in bed, instead of standing here reading f***ing poetry.

❧

The Streaker

I want to streak
the corridors
of your mind,
barefoot my heart,
naked my soul,
and light
the shadowed corners there
with a lamp of love.

❦

Dead Sea Scrolls

High up in this dry
and ancient cave
Will shepherds find clay jars
full of crumbling manuscripts?
Tiny fragments, brown with age,
mostly unreadable now,
even to me:
Lost love letters, never penned,
never sent to anyone who cared.

❦

Dance

Dance in the sun, dance 'neath the moon,
dance in the morning, dance at noon,
dance barefooted, dance in your shoes,
just put on whatever you choose.
Dance in clothing, dance in your skin,
leap with abandon, whirl and spin.
Dance has an energy all its own,
fills you with power in every bone.
Dance when your heart soars,
dance when the rain pours,
dance when your heart aches,
dance when your spirit breaks.
Dance when you're feeling good,
dance when misunderstood.
Dance when you have to cry,
dance when you want to die.
Dance when your hopes fade,
dance when you're most afraid.
Dance when you can't go on,
dance when your love is gone.
Dance till your heart stops,
dance till your body drops.
Dance till the Maker calls;
dance till the curtain falls.

❦

Letting Go

If measure of my love you'd
know, it's not in close embraces
found, nor in how long
I hold you so, how ardently
my arms surround. Instead it's
in my letting go: releasing you
without a sound, without a groan
or sigh to show how much
I'd rather keep you bound.

❦

Painted There

White clouds
on blue skies,
painted there
before your eyes.
Cool wind
and warm sun
come and go
as white clouds run
high up
in soft air.
White on blue,
Painted there.

❦

A Rose on the Beach

Upon the beach I found a lonely rose,
So perfect and unblemished in repose,
Its petals wet with dew from yesternight.
Forgotten in a moment of delight?
Or thrown away in sadness and despair?
What agonizing lover threw it there?

Or briefly did this lovely rose change hands,
Before being cast, rejected, on the sands?
Who tossed it here upon the sandy slope?
What fervent prayer, what frantic, burning hope
Died here between the sunset and the dawn,
Alive last night, and now forever gone?

So soon the waves will wash this rose away,
With all the hopes abandoned yesterday,
And some poor heart, remembering, now grieves
That every rose has thorns beneath its leaves.
But come a little closer; if you do,
Then thorns or no, I'll pluck a rose for you!

❦

The Garden of My Self
To Peggy, 10/20/92

Around my garden, years gone by,
I built a wall of stone, quite high.
And thus I kept intruders out,
with my great wall, so tall and stout.
But after many years I'd grown,
and found myself too much alone,
for now my flowers needed light—
and my old wall had too much height:
The wall that kept you far away
now kept me in, to my dismay.
So every time I felt alone,
I took away another stone
from off the wall around my heart
that used to keep us far apart.
And that way, slowly, inch by inch,
my wall became a garden bench.
So come into my garden, please,
enjoy its flowers and its trees.
My bench has lots of space to sit—
now won't you stay and talk a bit?

❦

Portal

Loving angels fly
to and fro through your smile:
Heaven's smallest gate.

❦

Hearts & Swords

There is no armor for the heart.
There's no protection from the pain
Of loving, losing, being apart,
Or loving someone all in vain.

I'll tell it from the very start,
Before I'd steel around my heart:
I met a girl with face so fair,
My need was more than I could bear.
And when she said she didn't care,
I vowed I'd never lose again,
I'd only love when I could win,
And I'd protect myself till then
By wearing steel around my heart.

If you surround your heart with steel,
Your heart will slowly start to rust,
And though the pain you may not feel,
Your heart will crumble into dust.

And now I'll tell the saddest part:
When I wore steel around my heart,
I met a girl much lovelier,
But felt no special love for her.
Yes, of that fact I was quite sure.
Yet, when she said her last goodbye,
I heard myself begin to cry,
And didn't know the reason why,
For I had steel around my heart. ➡

Hearts & Swords (cont'd.)

There is no science, is no art,
No way to safely shield your heart.
Don't hide your heart from pain and fright;
Your naked heart should shine more bright
Than swords gleam in mid-day light.
So never put your heart away,
Unsheathe your heart and let it say
Exactly what it feels today.
No, don't put steel around your heart.

There is no armor for the heart.
There's no protection from the pain
Of loving, losing, being apart,
Or loving someone all in vain.

❦

Perpetrators of Christmas newsletters often include parodies of famous poems, usually "A Visit From St. Nicholas." The meter is irregular, the rhymes wretched, and the theme trivial. Poe's "The Raven" has not, as far as I know, been thus abused...till now.

A Visit From the Christmas Maven

Once upon a midnight jolly,
weary from the Yuletide folly,
(decking halls with plastic holly,
rushing 'round from store to store,
attending parties overlapping,
present buying and present wrapping),
I sat down and started napping
'midst the holiday decor.

As I nodded, slowly slumping,
suddenly there came a bumping,
as of someone gently thumping,
thumping at my condo door.
I stood at the peephole, peeking.
"'Tis some drunk a party seeking,
with his breath of eggnog reeking,
this it is and nothing more."

On my doorstep stood a geezer:
hollow cheeks and purple beezer,
looked like he'd been in the freezer—
a hippie, from the clothes he wore:
Faded purple, long serape,
walking stick and sandals floppy,
purple hat and whiskers, sloppy—
all Salvation Army store.   ➡

A Visit From the Christmas Maven (cont'd.)

Laughing, I flung wide the portal,
prepared to have a little chortle,
at this poor, unfortunate mortal
standing at my condo door.
"You're a little early, Santa!
Come, I'll get out the decanter..."
'Fore I'd time for further banter,
"Santa" passed out on the floor.

Moistened washcloth on his forehead
brought him to, his cheeks much more red.
He then, sitting on the floor, said:
"Nick's my name. In days of yore,
Bishop Nick. Though now quite seedy,
I was rich, but never greedy,
gave my money to the needy,
presents to the very poor.

"Famous, once, from Bay of Fundy
to Cape Horn and back to Dundee...
Oh, sic transit gloria mundi!
Saint Nicholas you now ignore.
Santa's known to every Hotten-
Tot and Chinese, Indian, Scot, an'
Filipino—I'm forgotten!
It's Santa Claus you all adore!

"To the rich go Santa's presents,
spending little on the peasants,
thus you've lost the Christmas essence,
chasing after more and more.   ➼

A Visit From the Christmas Maven (cont'd.)

"That fat guy in the red suit, he
pushes toys and other booty,
shoes and gems and fashions snooty!
Gucci! Saks! Christian Dior!

"Beamers, boats and electronic
boxes blaring out moronic
network tripe in stereophonic,
knick-knacks, junk, and stuff galore.
Once a year I have a mission,
'fore the world goes to perdition,
to restore the old tradition,
make it like it was before!

"More religion and less business,
put some Christ back into Christmas,
on each continent and isthmus,
that's my self-appointed chore.
Now I think that I had best be
off. Thanks for the chance to rest me."
Nicholas got up and blessed me,
strode right through my condo door.

I awoke to sunlight beaming
on the decorations gleaming.
Surely, I'd been only dreaming,
dreaming of St. Nick, I swore.
Glad that we'd not been hobnobbing,
to relieve my headache throbbing,
I began my forehead swabbing
with the washcloth from the floor.

❦

The Operator

Somewhere deep inside me,
there's a telephone operator
who sits at the panel
where all my senses come
and routes the message to the right party
when I'm mad or glad, afraid or glum.
"Yes, Mr. Sudden Fear,
I'll connect you to Mr. Adrenals."
"I'm trying to reach Mr. Clench Fist
for Mr. Boiling Mad."
"Mr. Smile? I have Mr. Happy Moment
on the line."
"I have a call for Mr. Tear Ducts
from Mr. Feeling Sad."
The news was so bad one day,
she disconnected all the lines,
wiped her tears and moved to Alice Springs.
That was years and years ago—
and since then, I've hardly felt a thing.

❧

Anne

Winter on the beach—
cold waves splashing, roar and sigh.
Someone's far away.

❧

Slow Down

We're not really in any great hurry;
what's the rush, what's the worry?
Taking a break is apropos;
put it aside and let it all go.
Enjoy the moment, see the sky,
watch the clouds go sailing by.
Take a breath and let it out;
exhale worry, exhale doubt.
You deserve to take a rest,
get some troubles off your chest.
Tell me just how bad it seems,
Tell me all your hopes and dreams.
Get a kind word, get a hug;
here and now you're safe and snug.
So take some time to rest awhile
till you once again can smile.

❧

Someone

You remind me of one I know,
someone from years and years ago.
Someone with hair and eyes like you,
whose face and size and figure, too
were much like yours, my pretty doll.
I pray that someday, somehow, I'll
have you to love and kiss and hold,
and tell you what I wish I'd told
that girl of many years ago,
who never knew I loved her so.

❧

Wanted

I want the white moon to rise up tonight,
to shine down its silvery, primeval light.
I want the full moon to sail high above,
to help me to write you a poem of love.

I want blank paper as white as the moon,
a surface to carry my passionate tune.
I want jet ink as black as the night,
to tell you I love you in words that delight.

I want fine paper as fair as your skin,
to write out my heart-song for you once again.
I want an ink that's as dark as your hair,
to put down by moonlight just how much I care.

❦

The Hug

An embrace too brief:
faint nourishment for the heart—
dining on shadow.

❦

The Traveller

Grass hills right and left,
the green valley in Springtime
welcomes her lover.

❦

Time Capsule

I found today, full buried
in the grass in my backyard,
a baseball, weathered, grey,
and cracked with age,
and yet alive in spirit,
holding someone's memories
intact through years of hiding
dormant in the grass...
Nostalgia's rusty grip held me firmly,
transfixed in an instant of remembered
hours, minutes, days,
ticking off the happier times
of imagined sons and fathers
long away from this forgotten place,
where grass grows tall,
among the farthest flowers
in the corner of my heart.

❦

The Meteor

Fire in the sky:
lonely visitor from space
finds a home at last.

❦

Two, Not One

In the garden, by the roses
two butterflies flew across the path.
(Not one, two)

Sitting on the bench, I began
to wonder why I was here alone.
(One, not two)

And whether you, too, flew by
yourself, now,
(One, not two)

And whether someday we will fly
together as
One, not two.

❦

Tropical Heat

Hibiscus flower,
shaking in
the summer wind—
passion takes my heart

❦

Footsteps

Footsteps behind me in the dark...
Are they real? Do I hear
The click of steps a little out of time,
footsteps behind me in the dark?
Who is there? No one speaks.
My pace grows long, and, listening, I hear
footsteps behind me in the dark,
Dare I turn? Can I face
the nameless Fear that makes me hear the tread
of footsteps behind me in the dark?
Now I slow. So do they,
steps almost like an echo of my own,
Footsteps behind me in the dark.
Now I stop. Not a sound.
I turn to see the street behind me void.
No footsteps behind me in the dark.
Nothing there? But of course!
I really only thought I heard a noise
like footsteps behind me in the dark.
How absurd! How could I
imagine that there followed me tonight
footsteps behind me in the dark?
I walk on. And with this,
my body turns to ice because I hear
footsteps beside me in the dark.

❦

An Oyster to His Grain of Sand

I closed my shell too slowly once, and a particle of sand, which should have been swept away in the salty current, lodged inside me.

I closed my eyes too slowly, once, and your image, which should have been swept away in the crowd, lodged instead in my heart.

The tiny grain caused distress. I tried dissolving it, without success. A pearl built up around the sandy speck, but the pain went on.

Your memory evoked desire. I tried forgetting you, without success. Love built itself around your image layer after layer, but the pain continued.

One day, a diver split open my shell, smiled, and snicked out my pearl, then threw me back into the depths, empty, forgotten.

❦

Safety

I put my arms around you, once
And found I wasn't there.
I'd gone away to seek
A place of safety
Where I couldn't feel
Myself loving you.

❦

A Quiet Place

I found a very quiet place,
where silence stilled my soul,
where tranquil hours calmed my heart
and once more made it whole.

I found a cool and shadowed place,
among the laurel trees,
where all my troubles blew away
upon a gentle breeze.

I found a green, secluded spot,
beside a little stream,
and sat awhile, silently,
remembering a dream.

I dreamt of you the other night
(At least she seemed like you.)
Come join me in my quiet place—
there's room enough for two.

❦

Spring Windows

Outside my window, green and yellow trees
shake wet and shining leaves,
reminding me that I'm alive,
that I must dance the steps of Spring.
Against my window falls the rain,
running down the pane in rivers,
blurring my vision,
making a silent world shimmer and flow,
washing away my questions.
Over the windowsill flow the raindrops,
coursing down my cheeks,
falling to the floor in silence,
telling me to sleep somewhere
until my heart has healed.
Across my window, thin beams of sunlight
Sparkle through the raindrops,
giving me hope of a happier day,
sometime, when the sun will shine
again in my heart.

❧

The Stars in One Sky

Here and there about the sky are tiny lights—
Just cast an eye straight up and see them fill the dusk
in growing numbers till the black above is shot
with bright and dancing spots of purest white.

The void they fill is vast and cold, and never ends,
or so I'm told. But other voids, with other suns,
exist somewhere, although it stuns me just to think
of kinds of space that can't be found in any place
up there in our own starry skies, because our bodies
and our eyes have only length and width and height,
and so can't give us any sight of four or five dimension space.

And if, somehow, you turned to face dimensions
not among our three, perhaps in looking there you'd see
other worlds, with other men...Or parts of us beyond
our ken, because they are completely blind, or lie
where stars have never shined, where God in silence
occupies a universe of countless skies.

❧

Sunset

Magenta clouds
thrown across the sky
Sunset lingered
fading
a fantasy in red
a dying crimson dream
majestic in its slowly
coming end.
As the last color
slipped away
blue-black Night
brought down
a cold, dark
hand and
touched my heart.

❦

Tongue-tied

Why can't I say what I think?
I could do it as quick as a wink:
just three words would do, to say...
(Why can't I say what I think?)
Why can't I tell you right out?
I haven't the least bit of doubt.
If only you knew how much...
(Why can't I tell you right out?)
Why does my face turn so red?
And why am I silent instead
of telling you true, of how...
(Why does my face turn so red?)
Why can't I say it aloud,
instead of being hopelessly cowed?
It's nothing so new, it's just...
(Why can't I say it aloud?)
Why can't I summon up strength?
It wouldn't take any great length
to give you a clue to the fact...
(Why can't I summon up strength?)
Why can't I get to my feet,
the very next time that we meet,
when you come into view, to shout...
(Why can't I get to my feet?)
I think I know how to reveal
the tender emotion I feel:
a poem or two can say I love you!

❧

Mine

I found the serial number of the mine you
stepped on. I'm sorry. I know it's no
consolation. The medic tossed a twisted nugget
on my stretcher, flame-gnarled shrapnel stamped
0102011404151413051420
You may not care any more about words
or numbers or apologies. You took a step as
you told me you were going to rescue a comrade,
lying 1000 yards away.
Part of me needed to say, "don't go."
[step]...
Part of me admired your bravery
[click]...
Part of me feared you'd not make it back
[BOOM!]
That mine was 46 years old but still worked
too well. I don't remember much after that.
I think I heard another click...
I know that serial number.
I must admit
It was one of
Mine.

❦

Hesitation

Though lonely, somehow I cannot intrude,
beautiful girl, upon your solitude.

❦

Yellow Roses

Yellow roses grow within my heart for someone,
in a garden filled with flowers rare and sweet.
Leave your sandals by the gateway when you enter,
for the grass is always soft beneath your feet.

In the middle of my garden there's a fountain
in the sunlight, where the sparkling waters spray.
It's for you the crystal fountain makes its music,
it's for you the pulsing waters dance and play.

When you smile, there is sunshine in my garden,
when you laugh, the birds there fill the air with song.
When you touch me, then the garden turns to heaven;
you're my angel, in the place where you belong.

In the soft and gentle hours after twilight,
when the alabaster lanterns shed their glow,
in a safe, secluded corner of my garden,
I am waiting where the yellow roses grow.

❦

I Want to Be

I want to be the chest you lean your head upon.
I want to be the touch that wakes you up at dawn.
I want to be the voice upon your telephone.
I want to be the eyes that gaze into your own.
I want to be the hand that may caress your hair.
I want to be the heart you know will always care.
I want to be the arms that hold you tenderly.
I want to be the soft embrace that leaves you free.
I want to be the feet that walk along with you.
I want to be the one who loves you ever true.

❦

Tapestry

I wish I were woven into the tapestry of your life,
a part of the pattern sewn by the Fates long ago.
Beginning as thin golden threads among darkness,
I'd braid myself into the luster of happier times,
twined among silver threads of your laughter,
woven into the fabric of your smile,
glittering through the strands of your love,
To touch your heart forever, lover and friend.

❦

Golden Harbor Morning

In cool and quiet early morning darkness,
God's hand still turns the Earth beneath the stars,
till seabirds wake and fly along the shoreline,
to soar and cry a greeting to the dawn.

The sun illuminates the distant mountains
where purple peaks reveal a topaz sky;
and silver rays stream upward through the vapor
now scattering among the silent vales.

A brazen shield of sunlight on the ocean
reflects its hope on morning-brightened souls,
and newly-rising western winds blow strong
to fill again our slackened sails of dreams.

Oh, far off wind and water, ships and sailors,
bring hope across the deep blue ocean waves,
from foreign shores and unfamiliar places,
on shining seas, to this my harbor home!

❦

Springtime

Above, the fragrant blossoms fill the tree
For these young lovers...but not one for me.

❦

Timbukthree

Civilization wears me down
As I trudge from day to day
In a suit and tie either grey or brown...
How I long to run away!
Come, let us go where sea meets sky
Where the sun doth disappear.
We could both run amok and say goodbye
To our civilized veneer.
Off in the land of Timbukthree,
Where the natives go quite bare,
I would shed my suit by the boobah tree
And wear nothing whatsoe'er!
And when to Timbukthree we've come
We can do just as we please:
We can bay at the moon and pound the drum,
Underneath the boobah trees.
You'd doff your shoes and get undressed,
And run naked through the air—
Except when you dress in your Sunday best:
Boobah flowers in your hair.
Naked as aborigines,
When we live in Timbukthree,
We will swing on vines
through the boobah trees,
Free from all conformity.
Late, when the Timbuk moon is full
On the beach, all fancy-free,
We'll use for a drum
Each other's tum-tum—
Bouncing choreography.

❦

The Witch Who Came to Stay

I dreamt one night
a witch got in.
And having come,
didn't care to leave.
Who could tell a witch to go?
Who would even dare to?
So she stayed and stayed and
practiced her evil upon us.
When I woke up,
I still felt hopeless.

ॐ

Stepping Stone

Not every planet receives
a Moon
to agitate primordial seas,
to stir oceans of passion,
a Moon
to light the hunting-grounds
of Love.

Not every world
has a place to climb
when they've
run out of
mountains.

ॐ

Aunt Minerva Awakens

Auntie wants to rest in the shade,
dears, so you two play close by.
I'll read you a story later
No, don't go in the water just yet
Can you take off your suits?
Oh, no, that would not be proper.
Why not make a sand castle?
Can you bury me in the sand?
Well, I suppose so.

Such beautiful angels...
I wonder, will they be like me,
with orderly, sensible lives?
Or Gregory a sculptor, like his father,
Amanda an artist, like her mother?
They already show signs of talent.

So sleepy. I feel their small hands
patting cool sand over me,
mounding it upon my legs and body
as I lie here beneath the umbrella

Goodness. I must have dozed.
A pretty man passes by and smiles at me.
A new thing to me, being smiled at.
A second man walks along nearby.
He smiles at me, too, and now
I smile back, another new thing.   ➡

Aunt Minerva Awakens (cont'd.)

A couple plod across the sand.
He looks at me twice, then turns to her.
She sees me and laughs, eyes wide—
What makes her titter so?

I try to sit up but can't—
I'd quite forgotten being buried
I peer at the sandy shape
the "angels" have given me:
two huge breasts, with
pink seashells for nipples.
I know without looking,
beyond them lies a torso
like their mother's models,
in full and perfect detail.

Two naked imps giggle in unison.
I'd rise and swat their bare behinds,
but rising would destroy the
voluptuous body they've given me,
so different from my own,
which no one ever smiled at.

Another passerby covers his
mouth as he walks past.
I grin at him and we both laugh
But why are tears flowing?
I mustn't cry, lest the children
imagine it is they who've made me
so sad...and yet so alive.

❦

The Office "Poet"

People who write doggerel and pin it on the wall...
gall.
All they know of poetry is that it "ought to rhyme"
—a crime!
To force a rhyme, they take the words and
order them quite awkward—
Awss bawkward,
A feeble imitation of that man of odd panache
—Ogden Nash.
Meter only means to them a European length...
Give me strength!
Saying that they are poets should make Carl Sandberg...
feel slandered.
How I wish they'd take up free verse, where anything
goes, like the 900 word poem I saw that consisted of
the F-word written 899 times.

❦

Universe

Stars fill the cold sky
of millions, not one to match
the heart's full passion.

❦

Dark as Ink

In lonely darkness the poet can see
someone's tears were the first poetry.

"We Should Talk Sometime"

It would be good, yes,
to hear
your voice,
to hear your voice
from the farthest
orbit
of Jupiter. Does the Sun
shine bright
out there
amongst the seventy moons?
Or does it seem
just another star
in darkness
will our radios
hiss and pop and
whistle as we
listen on, perplexed?
Or will our messages each
ring strong and true?
Does such dixtanxe
lend enchxntmxnt,
or doex it merelx
rexult
in gxrblxd xignalx…
fadxng xwxy…
xnto…
xilenxe.
Ovxr xnd ouchchchchchchchch.......

❧

Hello, Hello

"Hello! Hello!" we'd say as we passed his cage,
and he'd hop towards us,
echoing: "Hello! Hello!"
"Goodbye! Goodbye!" we never taught him.
"Give us a ringie-dingie," we'd say,
and he'd mount the highest perch
and peck away at his silver bell.
Yesterday, behind the house,
I came across his empty cage,
and saw the little bell, silent
now for many years,
a few seeds and feathers
on the bottom of the cage,
from where his tiny form was lifted
on his last morning, small and still,
nevermore to ring the bell,
nevermore to say "Hello."

Goodbye, goodbye, little one!

❦

Five Hundred Goodbyes

Every time I left her in her last ten years,
I heard finality in my mother's goodbye,
a tone that said it might be
her last chance to say it.
And at her age it might have been.
Each time, I realized
that this might have been
our last visit, that there might be
something important left unspoken,
some unfinished business,
some unasked question
that she alone knew the answer to,
and a looming regret that I hadn't
stayed longer, come oftener,
talked more of old times, taken notes,
or said something to make her happier...
I only said goodbye to my father once.

❦

Tupelo

On one bright blue and sunny day,
'bout thirty years ago,
as I walked to the country store
outside of Tupelo,
I passed a young and pretty girl,
barefoot, small and shy.
She smiled at me and then looked down,
as I went walkin' by.

Barefoot girl, you're always in my heart,
even though we're miles and years apart.
Barefoot girl, I fell in love with you
long ago, and never even knew.

Oh, I was barely fourteen then,
and far too young to know
what all those feelings meant inside
that set my heart aglow.
I hurried to the store and got
the coffee and some thread,
but when I started back I saw
an empty road ahead.

As summer passed, I looked for her
along where she had been,
but never learned her name or saw
her pretty face again.
And as the summer days grew short,
and still we hadn't met,
I found my heart was carryin'
a mountain of regret.   ⇨

Tupelo (cont'd.)

Now many years have worn my heart,
and many days have flown,
but sometimes by the firelight,
when I am all alone,
or sometimes on a lonely night,
an hour 'fore the dawn,
I think of her and wonder where
that barefoot girl has gone.

I travel all around the world,
and everywhere I go,
imagine that I see her face,
so far from Tupelo.
I'd give the world to talk to her
and see that little grin,
but haven't any hope at all
we'll ever meet again.

❦

The Darkness

Last night
as twilight faded
I pulled shut
my bedroom curtains
making them go
shhhhh,
wishing me a quiet evening
I remembered then
the sound of curtains
from very long ago
as my mother went
from room
to room
closing them
hushhhh
hushhhh
hushhhh
holding back the darkness.

❦

The Autonomic Appraisal

The order of appraisal has a logic of its own, and it never
varies much:
I first survey the hair, and then the eyes, and face and lips.
I skip down to the feet, and slowly up the legs to scan the
hips, and, when the time permits, the breasts.

So, in the very instant I first saw you, began the process
automatic:
My glance caressed your hair, found it fine, and gravitated
to your eyes...

But when I reached your eyes, I fell in.
And now my heart swims naked, spinning unprotected in
the deep, dark amber whirlpools of your soul.

❦

May Morning

Blue-pink-yellow sky:
nature hides her eyes in mist—
naked, Summer comes!

❦

Call Of A Distant Song

As I awoke today at dawn, just as the sun was risin'
I heard the call of a distant song
upon my heart's horizon.

From somewhere far across the sea, from over hill
and heather, it seemed to say "Come away with me;
cast off your spirit's tether."

My heart's true home is calling, oh, across the endless
ocean. A nameless yearning tells me so,
a sad and strange emotion

"Away, away, come across the sea and over hill and
heather. Come, sing my song of spirits free
and hearts that beat together."

Alas, my duty chains me here, and others' expectations;
I cannot simply disappear, desert my obligations.

My day is done with all its cares, the dark of night
is falling, but still upon the twilight air
That distant song is calling.

❦

The Pearl

Iridescent sphere,
built around a source of pain:
the oyster's poem.

❦

SCROOGE

Now here is the story of Scrooge, Ebenezer
a very well known English financial geezer.
The reason for his fame, the cause of his renown?
Ebenezer Scrooge was the cheapest man in town!
Yes, though he was a rich man, the stories reveal
that Scrooge pinched his pennies with a grip of steel:
He wouldn't heat his office up when it was cold,
and went around the city with his boots half-soled.
His hankie wore out so he had someone patch it;
He downsized his firm to only Robert Cratchit.

He made poor Cratchit do the work of four,
and when the work was done, gave him even more.
He called Bob "management," to save another dime,
so he wouldn't have to pay any overtime.
The benefits were minimal, with stingy pay,
and never any savings plan or 401K.
When Bob asked for a raise, Ebenezer would swear,
and put a big phone book on top of Bob's chair.
Yes, Ebenezer Scrooge had little sympathy
for Bob, or his fam'ly, or Tiny Timothy.

But one dark evening as he figured what he grossed,
there came his partner, Marley, done up as a ghost:
Poor Marley wore chains and money boxes too;
and he clanked and he groaned and he looked very blue.
"Beware!" said Marley, "I've come to make you wiser
about what happens to a money-grubbing miser.
If *you* want your life not to be a total waste,
then *you* must reform and you'd better make haste." ⇨

SCROOGE (cont'd.)

"You're only a dream," Ebenezer told the ghost
"The effect of a chop or greasy bit of roast;
a nightmare sort of dream from a cheese gone stinky,
a rancid meatball or an out-of-date Twinkie."
Old Marley replied "You will end up just like me,
unless you are haunted by apparitions three."
Now, Scrooge didn't care for Marley's agenda,
but Marley just turned and vanished out the winda.

At one o'clock appeared the first Christmas shadow,
with Scrooge's knees knocking under his bravado.
The ghost said "Ebenezer, my name is Christmas Past.
I'll show how you were before your dough was amassed."
This ghost showed Mr. Scrooge his happy days of yore
and how his love of gold had slowly made him poor.
Old Ebenezer said "I am a wretch indeed!
I left the things I loved to better serve my greed."

'Twas later on that night when the next ghost appeared:
a jolly Christmas giant, not like Scrooge had feared.
The ghost said "Heard you say that I'm quite a humbug;
what most folks believe is: *you* are really scum, Bud.
I am the great and festive ghost-Christmas-present;
I'm here to show you things that are most unpleasant
about the careless way you treat your fellow man—
You can take some lessons from the Cratchit clan."
The ghost took Mr. Scrooge and showed him how it was
to live without money like the other guy does.
And Ebenezer said "Wow! Poverty's no joke.
An awful thing it is to be completely broke!"   ⇒

SCROOGE (cont'd.)

The next apparition was Christmas-Yet-To-Be.
Appearing at midnight, he beckoned silently.
"Lead on," said Mr. Scrooge, "I am yours to command."
The specter waved him on with a skeletal hand.
He showed Scrooge a future really, really grim:
A sad Cratchit household without a Tiny Tim.
He showed him an old tightwad who'd died all alone,
was buried in a grave with a marble headstone.

"They cried at his funeral? Not even a bit.
"His relatives all miss him? Quite the opposite?"
When Ebenezer asked "What's the name of this stooge?"
he was shown the inscription: "Ebenezer Scrooge!"

Now, Ebenezer woke at the sunlight's first gleam,
rejoiced to see that it all had been a dream.
He jumped out of bed and began to do a dance.
"That dream won't come true—I've got another chance!"
He called on his nephew to bury the hatchet,
ordered up a goose for Bob and Mrs. Cratchit.
And there was even more to his transformation:
the charity fund received a large donation.

Bob hadn't had a raise for ages and ages,
so Scrooge called him in, said "I'm raising your wages
to help you to improve your fam'ly's condition,
and let you take your Tim to a good physician.
"I was too proficient at grubbing after gold—
Controlling my destiny? I was *being* controlled!
Efficiency in business is all very swell,
but some things it's possible to do too well!"

❦

The Roller Coaster

I'm the One who designed the roller coaster, and I get more complaints than compliments:

You say the ride's too scary? You say you've tossed your popcorn and cotton candy, and the man next to you fell over the side, and the woman behind you stood up and got her head clipped off by a girder? And you say you want to get off?

Well, you were the one who got on board this thing. Yes, you were. You may not remember now, but you stood there watching the people all scream, And you said, "That's for me!' and clambered into the next little car.

Oh, you had a chance to get out. I offered you my hand, in case you wanted to get back onto cumulo-firma, But, no! You wanted to ride the roller coaster, you said. You wanted thrills and chills, you said.

And then the car began to move, not of your own volition, ascending with an ominous clack-clack-clack-clack-clack-clack-clack, and then it was too late.

Yes, you have to ride it to the end, now, down the sudden drops, through the left-right-left jerks, the up-and-down, stomach wrenching bumps, the swings from side to side that seem to go on forever.

Grab the bar tightly, lean into the curves, feel the car sway. Scream and yell 'WHEEEEEE!' as the scenery whizzes by. Feel the earth fall away from under you again and again.   ⇨

The Roller Coaster (cont'd)

And remember it's not real. I've got my hands around you, still:
My shiny steel tracks will hold you up, and my white-painted
timbers will not give way.

And your little car will keep moving, no matter what, down,
down, down, to where the track levels out, and you hear the
brakes hiss, and feel the car slow to the gentlest halt I could
design,
bringing you back to me safely,
as surely as I'm the One
who designed the roller coaster.

❦

Leaving Home

Goodbye is a word I won't say, tonight.
Hellos like ours shouldn't end in goodbye.
Instead of goodbye, can we say instead
Hello to the person you'll become?

Hello to the new places you're going,
and the new friends you'll meet there;.
Hello to the blessings God will send you
and the help you'll give others in return;

Hello to knowledge you'll find far away
and the wisdom you'll discover within,
Miles and miles away from here,
but not an inch from our hearts.

❦

Holding Hands

She reached for his
hand at the movies.
It seemed too good
to be true, at first.
Then he gloried in
the feel of her hand
in his. He held on
gently but silently,
feasting, not speaking,
Afraid it would end
too soon.

And when the film
was over,
they laughed
and sighed
and talked about
how wonderful it was,
the story,
the direction,
the cast.

Three score years from
now, he may not even
recall the plot.
What he'll remember is
her small hand,
unasked, remaining
in his grasp.

❦

Index

FUTURE PUBLICATIONS
WYZARD HILL PRESS

Excerpt: *The Perils of Tenirax,*
Mad Poet of Zaragoza (coming 2019)
Tenirax Strapped Down

A voice called out, full of morning enthusiasm, "Wakey-wakey!" Tenirax was not of that persuasion, preferring to greet the dawn only once it was well to the west of him.

¿Who is this lout that wakes a man at such an ungodly time of day, he wondered. There seems to be an echo, so I must be home in my little hideaway beneath the ruined chapel. But how did this rude oaf get in?

"*You're in the dungeon,*" a little voice said in his mind.

Suddenly remembering where he was, and why, Tenirax sat upright and opened his eyes to the horror that awaited him. There, beside the rack, was Bungorolo, already stripped to the waist and leather-aproned.

The torturer was raking hot coals from an iron scuttle into a large brazier beside the rack, humming a simple tune as he did so. He looked at Tenirax "Come! You must join me." Bungorolo opened the cell door and helped the poet to his feet.

"I'd rather stay in here, if you don't mind." Tenirax shivered.

"Nonsense. It's much warmer out here. Have a seat. Warm yourself." The torturer indicated the rack and brazier.

Tenirax hobbled over to the rack and cautiously sat on the edge, expecting at any moment to be grabbed and forcibly strapped in place. He noted Bungorolo's beefy arms, bigger than his own thighs, and estimated how many seconds lay between him and profound agony. Perhaps as few as ten, he thought.

Bungorolo reached out a hand, and Tenirax recoiled in utmost fear. But Bungorolo merely bent down and pulled a grille from beneath the rack, then placed it across the brazier, followed by a small pan. Soon, the aroma of frying eggs and a bit of meat met Tenirax's nose.

"Want some?" the torturer asked.

"Not hungry," was all Tenirax could manage to say.

❦

Excerpt: *Sail Away on My Silver Dream* (2018)
Chapter 1: Clouds

The first scary thing happened on Saturday, a week before school started. It was really hot that day. I was in the back yard, using the weed trimmer and getting all sweaty and covered with shredded grass. Mom had her long, brown hair done up in a bandana and was wearing her grubby jeans, cutting roses beside the garden shed. I saw her straighten up, and then she dropped her clippers and just stood there like a statue. Something was wrong with the way she was standing. I stopped what I was doing and wondered, *what's the matter with Mom?*

❦

Excerpt: *In the Mouth of the Lion*
(now available)

The German spoke. "Dr. Jung, I come on the behalf of my employer, Mr. Wolff, who desperately needs the kind of healing you specialize in."

Jung waved the idea away. "My practice is closed. I am taking no new clients..."

The man became less confident. "Perhaps if you heard some of the details—"

Jung was tempted to ask him to explain, but fear overruled his curiosity. "No, no. I am not interested."

"Please, Herr Dr. Jung. Mr. Wolff has met you and wants you in particular."

"We have met? I don't recall a 'Mr. Wolff.' Who is this Mr. Wolff?"

The German leaned back and folded his arms across his chest. "Adolf Hitler."

❦

Excerpt: *Sorcerer of Deathbird Mountain*
(coming in 2019)

Lord Vinifer, Chancellor of the city of Cis Brogundo, scurried along the palace corridor towards King Strogulus's chambers. He was breathing heavily by the time the guard threw open the heavy oak door to admit him, but the frown on his aged face was unrelenting.

He slammed the door behind him. "Sire!" he wheezed before pausing to breathe.

The king was sitting on the edge of his canopied bed, eating breakfast. "Ho, Vinifer. What is it now?" he said, looking up from his tray. "Can't it wait until later?" He looked back at the sausage on his plate.

The tall chancellor leaned down and put both hands on the nearest table to steady himself. Unable to speak from lack of breath, he answered with an emphatic shake of his head.

The king put down his knife and fork and thrust his silver goblet in the old man's direction. "Have some mead, Vinifer, and speak."

Vinifer ignored the goblet. He gasped, "It's . . . it's Zeundrom, Sire! He . . . he's . . . gone!"

King Strogulus stood abruptly, spilling his tray. "Zeundrom? Our wizard? Gone? You mean . . . "

Vinifer nodded. "Dead, Sire, yes." He straightened and adjusted his robes, attempting to regain some dignity.

"You're sure?"

"Perfectly sure. I verified his death myself. He's quite dead, Sire."

❧

EXCERPT: *SHERLOCK AND THE TWELVE APOSTLES*
(COMING IN 2019)

I heard footsteps slowly ascending the stairs. "Hark, Watson!" said Holmes. "Who would this be?"

"I was just thinking of retiring."

"Wait a bit, Watson. Let's see what our visitor wants." Holmes took a puff on his pipe and looked towards the door. "He's an elderly clergyman, and he very likely wishes to borrow money."

"Shall I tell him to go away, then?" I must confess I was more interested in sleep than mystery.

"No, no, Watson. He would like to consult us on a disturbing or awkward matter. Let him in, would you?"

I opened the door and startled an elderly man in a clerical collar, fist already raised to knock. "Are you Mr. Sherlock Holmes?" he asked. His voice was deep and resonant, far more stentorian than I'd expected from such an elderly man.

"I'm Dr. John Watson. Who shall I say is calling?"

"I'm Fr. Francis Habakkuk of St. Rupert's Church," he said, "and I'm dreadfully embarrassed to ask, but could I prevail upon your Christian charity to borrow sixpence? I'm afraid I'm short on the cab fare."

I found the necessary coin and handed it to him. As he slowly descended the stairs, I turned to Holmes. "Once again, you've got me almost completely baffled. How did you know he'd be a needy cleric? Elementary, I presume, but I still must hear it."

❦

Excerpt: *Something Wicked in Ichekaw* (coming in 2019)

Sheriff Del Singletary looked across at the Regulator clock on the wall above the gun rack. The brass pendulum was slowly ticking off the last minute before the hour hand touched six. Singletary drew his booted feet off the big oak desk, stood, and rolled up his revolver in its leather gun belt before shoving it into the bottom drawer. He put on his heavy, crimson-and-black checkered hunting jacket and his black Stetson, then bent down by the big front window to turn the sign to CLOSED. "Well, that's enough shit for one day," he said, standing up and stretching to his full six foot four.

A red pickup truck screeched to a halt outside. As it rocked back on its springs, Sheriff Singletary saw a flash. A hole appeared in the window in front of him, and something struck him in the chest like an invisible fist. He staggered, steadied himself, then lunged toward the gun rack, reaching for the nearest lever action Winchester. He could hear the window shatter and more shots being fired, but ignored everything except the pain in his chest and the nearest rifle. As blackness engulfed him, Singletary fell to the gritty, bare wooden floor, dead before the last shard fell from the window pane.

❦

Excerpt: *Out Brief Candelle* (2019)

BOOM! BOOM! BOOM! Far away, a fist pounded on a door. *An oaken door*, he thought. *Heavy, 'tis, with sturdy, black-iron hinges...*

H*oy! 'Tis my door*, Quynt Quayne thought, finally waking. *That is someone downstairs at my door, not far away; 'tis a pity.* He opened his eyes and looked towards the clock at the foot of his sleeping cubicle. A phosphorescent "3" glowed faintly through the opening in the clock face. *Three of the clock. 'Tis the middle of the flacking night. They must want me to snuff someone. By the four kings, I really need to find better work.*

❦

A Final Note

I hope you've enjoyed this edition of *Poems of Nostromo*. It was fun to revisit these works and make a few updates, as needed.

But it's a fact that having written a book is more fun than writing it. And one of the very best parts of having written a book is hearing from the people who enjoyed it! Please let me hear from you.

Better than that, even, is when readers tell other people they liked my book, either by word of mouth or in the form of a review on their favorite book discussion website. Please be one of my angels and post a review. It doesn't have to be very long.

Biography

J Guenther is a graduate of the University of Southern California, with BS and MS degrees in engineering. He has written 22 stage plays, three computer books, four magazine articles, 50 short stories, five novels and many poems. His classical three-act play, *Midnight in the Temple of Isis*, and many of his shorter works for the stage have been performed in theaters from Los Angeles to Santa Barbara. *Prisoner of Suggins Holler* was a prize winner in Elite Theatre Company's 2010 One-Act Play Contest. His fantasy book, *Sorcerer of Deathbird Mountain*, was nominated for best novel at the Santa Barbara Writers Conference in 2005.

Jeff's general site for his writing is:
https://jguentherauthor.wordpress.com/

www.ingramcontent.com/pod-product-compliance
Lightning Source LLC
Chambersburg PA
CBHW021204020426
42331CB00003B/198

* 9 7 8 0 9 9 7 4 5 0 3 4 7 *